Is Atlantis Real?

BY ALLISON LASSIEUR

AMICUS HIGH INTEREST ✦ AMICUS INK

Amicus High Interest and Amicus Ink are imprints of Amicus
P.O. Box 1329, Mankato, MN 56002
www.amicuspublishing.us

Library of Congress Cataloging-in-Publication Data
Lassieur, Allison.
 Is Atlantis real? / by Allison Lassieur.
     pages cm. – (Unexplained : what's the evidence?)
 Includes bibliographical references and index.
 Summary: "Presents the story of the lost city of Atlantis and
examines discoveries that are claimed to be Atlantis, ultimately
stating there is no hard proof that Atlantis existed"– Provided by
publisher.
 ISBN 978-1-60753-802-8 (library binding) –
 ISBN 978-1-60753-891-2 (ebook)
 ISBN 978-1-68152-043-8 (paperback)
 1. Atlantis (Legendary place)–Juvenile literature. I. Title.
 GN751.L37 2016
 398.23'4–dc23
                                          2014033283

Editor   Rebecca Glaser
Series Designer   Kathleen Petelinsek
Book Designer   Heather Dreisbach
Photo Researcher Derek Brown

Photo Credits: Cover; Dorling Kindersley/Getty Images, 5;
Lee Walters/Alamy, 6; Juancat/Shutterstock, 9; Hemis/Alamy,
Brigida Sorino/Shutterstock 10; SOBERKA Richard/Hemis/
Corbis, 13; Thomas Aichinger/imagebroker/imageBROKER,
14; imageBROKER/Alamy, 17; Rod Haestier/Alamy, 18;
The Helike Project/Dora Katsonopoulou, 21; FLPA/Alamy,
22; imageBROKER/Alamy, 25; Ancient Art & Architecture
Collection Ltd/Alamy, 26; Erik Simonsen/Getty Images, 29

Printed in Malaysia

HC 10 9 8 7 6 5 4 3 2 1
PB 10 9 8 7 6 5 4 3 2 1

Table of Contents

WITHDRAWN

What Is Atlantis?

Long ago, there was a story about a beautiful city called Atlantis. It was on a huge island. It had tall walls. In the middle was a huge **temple** made of gold and silver. It was filled with hundreds of golden statues. The island was rich. They had good crops. For years, the people lived in peace.

The temple in Atlantis was surrounded by rings of water.

The stories say Poseidon was the first ruler of Atlantis.

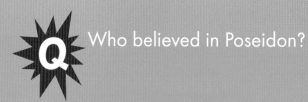

Q Who believed in Poseidon?

In the story, Atlantis belonged to the god **Poseidon**. He fell in love with a human woman named Cleito. They had ten sons. The sons were part god and part human. Each son ruled a part of Atlantis. They were strong, beautiful, and smart. They had many children. The city grew.

 The **ancient** Greeks. In Greek myths, Poseidon was the Greek god of the sea and earthquakes.

Many years passed. The people of Atlantis started a war. Poseidon was not happy. So one day, he made an earthquake hit Atlantis. The land shook. A huge **volcano** erupted. In only one day, the island sank under the water. Since then, people have told the story of Atlantis. Most people think it is a myth. Others say it could be true.

In the story, a volcano sank Atlantis.

9

This statue of Plato stands in Greece. It is near a school he started, called the Academy.

Q When did Plato write about Atlantis?

Stories and Searching

We know about Atlantis because of Plato. Plato was a great thinker from ancient Greece. He heard the story of Atlantis and wrote it down. He said it was real. People were amazed by the stories of gold and wealth. Was Plato right about Atlantis? No one could prove it. But maybe he based the story on a real city.

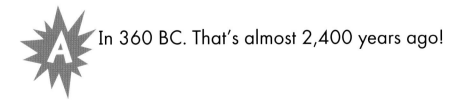 In 360 BC. That's almost 2,400 years ago!

The story of Atlantis is very old. It was told many times. But it became popular in the late 1800s. Atlantis showed up in novels. A man named Ignatius Donnelly had many ideas about the lost city. He wrote a book. He said the people of Atlantis were very smart. He said the island was in the Atlantic Ocean. Many people read his book.

People are fascinated by the
mysteries of ancient cities.

A scuba diver explores ruins in a lake in Italy.

 Q What does a marine archaeologist do?

Many people have looked for Atlantis. Other ancient cities have been lost, too. Some of them are now deep under the sea. **Marine archaeologists** look for lost cities on the ocean floor. They may find parts of buildings. They may find pieces of art and pottery. One of these underwater cities could be Atlantis.

 They look for man-made objects in the ocean. They study shipwrecks and ruins.

The Minoans

In 1900, an archaeologist found a real lost city. Sir Arthur Evans dug at a site on the island of Crete. He found ancient ruins. There were beautiful palaces and buildings. The people who lived there must have been smart, powerful, and strong. Evans called them Minoans. Plato could have based the story of Atlantis on these people.

These ruins are on the island of Thera. Minoans lived there.

Why was the Minoan city in ruins? Miles away was an island called Thera. Minoans had a city there, too, near a huge volcano. Around 1500 BC, it blew apart! It shook the earth. Ash filled the air. A big chunk of Thera sank into the ocean. The eruption made a **tsunami** that was so big it reached Crete. The Minoans were destroyed.

A tsunami creates waves that can destroy towns near oceans.

Other Lost Cities

Helike (HEH-lee-kee) was an ancient Greek city. A huge earthquake and tsunami destroyed it. It sank into a swamp. But parts of the city stuck up out of the water. Over the years the water filled up with **silt**. The silt buried everything. Helike was forgotten. Scientists found it in 2001. But they did not find it underwater. They found it underground.

The ruins of Helike were found underground in southern Greece.

This swampy park in Spain covers a lost city.

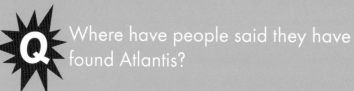

Q Where have people said they have found Atlantis?

Another lost city was found in Spain in 2011. It was underwater in a park. The lost city has walls like Atlantis. In 2012, scientists found something underwater near Scotland. It was an area where many people once lived. Some people thought it could be Atlantis. But Spain and Scotland are far from Greece. Plato may not have heard of them.

 At the North Pole, in South America, and even in Antarctica!

What's the Evidence?

There is no real proof that any lost city was Atlantis. Today most people do not believe the story. They don't think Atlantis was real. Other people think part of Plato's story might be true. He might have heard about a real city. Plato could have used some real facts and made up others. So far, no lost city matches all the facts in Plato's story.

People built fake ruins of Atlantis. Tourists can visit the Hotel Atlantis in Dubai.

Two lost cities are more likely than others. One is Thera. But Plato said Atlantis sank 9,000 years before he wrote the story. The volcano at Thera blew up thousands of years later. Maybe Plato got the date wrong. The other is Helike. It was destroyed by an earthquake and tsunami in 373 BC. Plato was alive then. Maybe he based the story on this town.

This Minoan art was found on a wall in Thera.

27

Plato's Atlantis was a great city. If it was real, it would be amazing to find it. Today, archaeologists can use new tools. **Sonar** can find objects in deep water. **Satellites** in space take pictures of Earth's surface. Archaeologists try to match the pictures to Plato's story. But so far, Atlantis is still a mystery.

Satellite pictures of Earth's surface may help people find ancient cities.

Glossary

ancient Very old; having lived or existed for a long time.

marine archaeologist A person who studies the past by looking for old buildings and objects at the bottom of the ocean.

Poseidon In Greek mythology, the god of the sea and earthquakes.

satellite A machine that is sent into space and circles around Earth; some satellites take pictures.

silt Fine sand carried by water that fills an area.

sonar A device that can find objects deep underwater using sound waves.

temple A building for the worship of a god.

tsunami A gigantic ocean wave caused by an earthquake that can cause great destruction when it reaches land.

volcano A hole in the earth's crust where lava and steam erupt.

Read More

Karst, Ken. *Atlantis.* Mankato, Minn.: Creative Education, 2014.

Martin, Michael. *The Unsolved Mystery of Atlantis.* North Mankato, Minn.: Capstone Press, 2014.

Owings, Lisa. *Atlantis.* Minneapolis, Minn.: Bellwether Media, Inc., 2015.

Websites

Easy Science for Kids:
All About the Lost City of Atlantis
easyscienceforkids.com/all-about-the-lost-city-of-atlantis/

Kidz World: History: The Lost City of Atlantis
www.kidzworld.com/article/960-history-the-lost-city-of-atlantis

National Geographic: Atlantis:
True Story or Cautionary Tale?
science.nationalgeographic.com/science/archaeology/atlantis/

Index

About the Author

Allison Lassieur loves reading and writing about strange, mysterious, and unusual places in the world. She has written more than 150 books for kids, and she also likes to write about history, food, and science. Allison lives in a house in the woods with her husband, daughter, three dogs, two cats, and a blue fish named Marmalade.